A Leap Year of Limericks

A Leap Year of Limericks

David Fletcher

Copyright © 2020 David Fletcher

The moral right of the author has been asserted.

Apart from any fair dealing for the purposes of research or private study, or criticism or review, as permitted under the Copyright, Designs and Patents Act 1988, this publication may only be reproduced, stored or transmitted, in any form or by any means, with the prior permission in writing of the publishers, or in the case of reprographic reproduction in accordance with the terms of licences issued by the Copyright Licensing Agency. Enquiries concerning reproduction outside those terms should be sent to the publishers.

This is a work of fiction. Names, characters, businesses, places, events and incidents are either the products of the author's imagination or used in a fictitious manner. Any resemblance to actual persons, living or dead, or actual events is purely coincidental.

Matador
9 Priory Business Park,
Wistow Road, Kibworth Beauchamp,
Leicestershire. LE8 0RX
Tel: 0116 279 2299
Email: books@troubador.co.uk
Web: www.troubador.co.uk/matador
Twitter: @matadorbooks

ISBN 978 1838593 599

British Library Cataloguing in Publication Data.
A catalogue record for this book is available from the British Library.

Printed and bound in the UK by TJ International, Padstow, Cornwall
Typeset in 11pt Sabon MT by Troubador Publishing Ltd, Leicester, UK

Matador is an imprint of Troubador Publishing Ltd

There was a young girl named Simone
Who learnt a new use for her phone
It was lots of fun
But in more ways than one
It did rather bring down the tone

*

There was a young man called De Croix
Who was famed for the length of his *bois*
It extended so far
It would quite often star
As the lead in a *ménage à trois*

*

There was a young woman who saw
Her own husband procuring a whore
Well, unlike his grief
The procurement was brief
And so was the punch to his jaw

*

There was a young fellow called Tone
For whom girls were a virtual unknown
He was often attacked
For the sex that he lacked
But he'd learnt how to well hold his own

There was a young girl who was taught
That a sailor was worth less than nought
Oh, but strong rating Roy
And the shudder of joy
When his vessel docked in her home port!

*

There was a young girl who had sussed
That her principal draw was her bust
And she soon got to know
How to put it on show
With the help of a bra she could trust

*

There is a young woman called Joan
Who weighs in at eighty-eight stone
She once had a chap
(who went in with a map)
Whose location is now an unknown

*

There once was a man who relied
On a method much trusted and tried
When out on a date
He'd just ask for it straight
And if that didn't work, he just cried

There was a young chappie called Harris
With a warhead the size of Polaris
And one hardly need say
That when brought into play
It would harden like plaster of Paris

*

There was a young girl from Port Rush
Who had grown the most beautiful bush
And just to be clear
What we're talking 'bout here
Is the sort that you'd prune and not brush

*

There once was a fellow from Lima
Who was known for the size of his steamer
In fact, I recall
That if measured 'with ball'
It was almost as long as his femur…

*

There was a young man who suggested
His wife should be much bigger breasted
This advice was ill-thought
And I have to report
The divorce, it will not be contested

Young Jason was quite large below
But he knew there was some way to go
So, with infinite care
What he nurtured down there
In the end won the prized 'best in show'

*

Young Edna liked custard and jelly
And most of the rubbish on telly
But what she liked more
Was to be on the floor
With a man bearing down on her belly

*

There was a young girl called Kincaid
Who took up a job as a maid
Her duties were light
But I hear every night
That her legs ended up widely splayed

*

There was a young fellow called Jake
Whose pride was his single-eyed snake
It was often at rest
But when put to the test
It could rise up and make women quake

There once was a lady whose backside
Was a little too much on the slack side
So she joined a small gym
For her bum so to slim
But her zeal was soon swapped for a backslide

*

There was a young lady called Jade
Whose appearance was sober and staid
But under that crust
Was a whole lot of lust
And a G-string of finely rubbed suede

*

There was a young fellow called Bonaparte
Who once tried to take his smart phone apart
But his being a dunce
It exploded at once
And that's how his balls they were blown apart

*

There was a young man from Dunedin
Who once lost his licence for speedin'
And the losses went on
When his transport had gone
Coz he then lost the pot that he'd peed in

There was a young actor from Derby
Who just knew that one day he'd a star be
But his dreams came to nought
When one night he was caught
With a full-size inflatable Barbie

*

There was a young fellow called Porter
Who fancied an alchemist's daughter
He wanted to hold her
And tightly enfold her
But more so to pestle her mortar

*

There was a young lady called Bess
Who quite simply drank to excess
And when she was tight
She would often invite
Different men to have fun up her dress

*

There was a young yeoman called Paul
Whose codpiece was desperately small
Yes, of room for his stuff
There was not quite enough
…so outside it hung one lonely ball

There was a young lady called Nicky
Who, with boyfriends, was not very picky
But much worse than this
Was, instead of a kiss
She'd quite often give them a quickie

*

There was a young tart called Marie
Who wanted more business, you see
So her calling card said
'If you take me to bed
You can try one and get one for free'

*

There was a young man who would find
That he thought about sex as he dined
And the bigger the meal
Then the more that he'd feel
That he needed a (non-pepper) grind

*

There once was a fellow called Billy
Whose libido was just like Caerphilly
And that is to say
It soon crumbled away
And had little to do with his willy

There was a young girl called Atari
Who married a young, rich Qatari
It has to be said
He was piss-poor in bed
But he did own a big red Ferrari

*

There was a young chappie from Dallas
Who was noted for being quite callous
He was also a dick
As in 'prize-winning prick'
So they called him the 'mean-minded phallus'

*

There was a young woman called Linda
Who slept with a guy called Mahinder
Well, believe it or not
Our Lin was so hot
That his todger got burnt to a cinder

*

There was a young fellow called Janic
Whose member was truly titanic
And just like that ship
When it 'went for a dip'
Its sinking could cause quite a panic

There was a young fellow called Sawyer
Who worked as a high-flying lawyer
But back on the ground
He just slithered around
In pursuit of his role as a voyeur

*

There was a young lady from Harrow
Who sold fruit and veg from a barrow
She married a man
(who sold from his van)
When she saw the huge size of his marrow

*

There was a young lassie from Lauder
Whose knickers were well out of order
They all failed to hide
What was lying inside
Coz they needed their gussets made broader

*

There was a young girl called Glendower
Who quite often peed in the shower
And over a year
I'll tell you, my dear
It saved her well over an hour

There was a keen lover named Claude
Whose technique with women was flawed
And that's why, you see
He had turned sixty-three
By the time he had finally scored

*

There was a young lady called Lulu
Who quite often wore a pink tutu
But that's *all* she would wear
Which is why, I declare
Its pink matched the pink of her fufu

*

There was a young woman called Jane
Whose knickers were patterned not plain
With shorts that were white
And worn very tight
This choice was quite hard to explain

*

There was a young chappie from Crewe
Who of todgers had no less than two
So for years he looked out
For a girl kitted out
With a rare but compatible flue

There was a young chappie from Brighton
Whose balls would his girlfriends quite frighten
They did used to say
That his brother's were grey
But he had one green an' one white 'un

*

There was a young man from Hong Kong
Who was blessed with a sizable schlong
So he took the full blame
For the fall-out that came
When he housed it in just a small thong

*

There once was a woman called Hilda
Who fell for a bloke from St Kilda
She so loved his looks
And his interest in books
And his part that so frequently filled her

*

The true love of Archibald Victor
Was elated when Archie first picked her
But when Archie's 'romance'
Sank to 'take off yer pants'
She began to believe that he'd tricked her

There was a young chappie called Howard
Who quite often seriously glowered
The reason he did
Was a geezer called Sid
And the girlfriend who Sid had deflowered

*

There was a young girl from Bombay
Who fancied a pilot called Ray
She loved to be flown
– just the two on their own
And a joystick with which she could play

*

There is an old woman from Bude
Who pays to be slowly shampooed
(Not the hair on her head
And the purpose, it's said
Is to get the old girl in the mood)

*

There was a young chap from Long Lartin
Whose car was a blue Aston Martin
And an orgy for two
In his Aston so blue
Was what he so loved to take part in

There was a young lady called Suzy
Who was known as a bit of a floozy
And by that I mean, folks
That in choosing her blokes
She was anything other than choosey

*

There is an old fellow from Stornoway
Whose penis has more or less worn away
Yes, its use in the past
Has made it not last
And our 'Tearaway Jock' is now 'Torn-away'

*

There was a young girl from Kuwait
Who felled trees with the help of a mate
Six in a day
She could cope with OK
But she'd choke if she had to fell_eight

*

There was a young woman called Tess
Who kept falling out of her dress
The reason perhaps
Was, regarding her baps
She'd been showered with too much largesse

There was a young lady called Julie
Whose behaviour was often unruly
Which is why at a dance
She once grabbed a guy's pants
And discovered he'd only one goolie

*

There was a young lady called Chloe
Who decided to wax her below-ee
But the wax was all wrong
And the hair grew back strong
So that Chloe then needed a mow-ee

*

There was a young woman who wed
And thereafter did share her own bed
And whilst not a ball
What she feared most of all
Was the rise of the dread purple head

*

There was a young girl who was Greek
And who thought of herself as quite chic
Well, she did have a case
But there was then her face
(and the landscape downstairs was quite bleak)

There was a young fellow called Bryant
Whose todger was no less than giant
It was so bloody big
That it needed a jig
For its use to be EU compliant

*

As Louise's libido got higher
She would quickly remove her attire
She was so bloody hot
That if she did not
The risk was her pants would catch fire

*

There once was a good-natured tart
Whose thighs were set quite well apart
With this kindness and gap
She attracted a chap
And in due course she captured his heart

*

Young Mary could only astound
With her swimsuit the wrong way around
Her boobs were on show
And just down below
Was a risk of 'exposure of mound'

There was a young girl called Nigella
Who liked outdoor sex with her fella
They'd have it away
On the lawn every day
And if raining they'd use an umbrella

*

There was a young love child who found
That she much liked her hands to be bound
But it didn't go right
On one water-bed night
When a burst meant she ended up drowned

*

There was a big girl, Sarah Jane
Whose bras had a lot to contain
In fact, one could say
They were stressed every day
– with those forty-two pounds to restrain

*

There was a young laddie called Warren
Who was weird and decidedly foreign
He ate thistle stew
Said 'Och aye the noo'
And his scrotum he kept in his sporran

There was this young lady stunt flier
Whose aircraft on one day caught fire
She then used her chute
Which was fine, my old fruit
Til she landed astride a church spire

*

There was a young fellow called Hywel
Who was supposedly hung like a mule
And this assertion was true
As one concierge knew
When he entered her large vestibule

*

There was a young man from Kirkuk
Who quite often got himself stuck
This was in the sex act
And was due to the fact
That his todger was shaped like a hook

*

There was a young girl who would laugh
At a miner she thought was real daft
But the laughs had to go
When she looked down below
And first saw the huge size of his shaft

There was a young woman called Sophie
Whose whatsit had won her a trophy
One has to deduce
That she charged for its use
And the fee charged was far from a low fee

*

There was a young lass called Louise
Whose purpose in life was to please
What that more often meant
With her boyfriends she spent
A great deal of time on her knees

*

There was a young fellow called Rory
Who was set up for fame, wealth and glory
But some weird 'ow's yer father
(plus one lost cadaver)
Delivered a quite different story

*

There was a young lady from Weston
Who was open to any suggestion
She was almost hard-wired
To give *more* than desired
But she'd always perform with her vest on

Ever since Bernard had shaved
He'd been decent and so well behaved
But when he reached forty
He got very naughty
(in fact, he got really depraved)

*

There was a young man from Penzance
Who embarked on a thought-out advance
His target was Kate
And by quarter past eight
He'd attacked and then taken her pants

*

There was a young woman from Rhyl
Who was blessed with an uncommon skill
She would take off her clothes
And when in the right pose
With her buttocks then break a brazil

*

There was an old guy who would boast
That he'd once screwed a rather stiff ghost
The truth of the fact
Was he'd done a sex act
With a hole in a half-hidden post

There was a young fellow called Shand
Whose night out was not as he'd planned
But that was before
He had met this nice whore
Who very soon took him in hand

*

There was a young woman from Haifa
Who looked like a young Michelle Pfeiffer
And as well as her face
Her body was ace
And her butt was a butt just to die for

*

There was a young man from Penrith
Who claimed that gay love was a myth
But when he moved in
With a guy called Gay Glynn
We all knew he'd been taking the pith

*

There was a young man who was found
On a golf course, laid out on the ground
He'd been hit on the head
By the woman he'd wed
When she found he'd been playing a_round

There was a young girl called Yvette
Who won a ten-million pound bet
As she wanted to try
Being bonked a mile high
She then purchased her own private jet

*

There was a young woman called Lisa
Whose husband knew well how to please her
And all it would take
Was a milk-chocolate flake
And the use of a nearby chest freezer

*

There was a young girl from Hanoi
Who wore pants made from thick corduroy
Forget women's lib
– with that vertical rib
They made for a firm source of joy

*

There was a young woman called Rita
Who drove a nice open two-seater
Of its cylinders' size
She was sadly not wise
But she did know her own was one litre

There was a famed caver named Joe
Who would give any cavern a go
And as many girls found
(when not underground)
He really was big down below

*

There was a young gymnast from Malta
Who fell for an archer called Walter
Their sex life was great
Coz Walt's aim was first rate
And she was a prize-winning vaulter

*

There once was a woman from Cuba
Who settled with wealth in Aruba
Her fortune she'd made
With the loot she'd been paid
For designing the world's best de-puber

*

There was a young pervert called Bill
Who upset a lady called Jill
What he did was dispose
Of both his and her clothes
And then hold her against his/her will

There was a young woman from Hobart
Who in Tonga was hit by a blow dart
And that's why, they say,
When it comes to a lay
She quite often makes quite a slow start

*

There was a young chappie from Troon
Who was known as the human harpoon
So long was his 'spear'
That when women came near
They'd either go mad or they'd swoon

*

There was a young woman from Deal
Who herself she would quite often feel
She quite liked her tum
And she did love her bum
But her top spot was always her keel

*

A young lover from Sweden called Liv
Had a mind that was just like a sieve
Did one thrust, pump or grind
Who took whom from behind
And with head, did one take or just give?

There was a young 'dancer' called Delia
Whose stage name was 'Lusting Lobelia'
For ten pounds she'd go
For five she'd just blow
And for one pound she'd no more than feel ya

*

Kim's sex life was mostly OK
But it did lack a certain *Ole!*
Then Kim got converted
To acts quite perverted
And now it's *Ole!* every day…

*

There was a young girlie called Boeing
Whose pastimes were knitting and sewing
But an interest in boys
And in adult powered toys
Could soon be observed to be growing

*

There was a young lady called Tracey
Who defined what it meant to be racy
Her tops were worn taut
Her skirts very short
And her pants were invariably lacy

There was a young man called John Dee
Who of testes had no less than three
One was hirsute
The second quite cute
And the third played The Rose of Tralee

*

There was a young girl with an arse
That looked like the famed Khyber Pass
But despite this odd rear
I'll tell you, my dear
That in bed she was always first class

*

There was a young woman who skated
Round a topic quite often debated
And the topic is still:
'If one's seeking a thrill
Should one's gusset be made corrugated?'

*

There was a young woman called Laughton
Who had one long teat and one short 'un
The short was the best
Coz it so matched its breast
And it wasn't the one with the wart on

There was a young fellow from Troon
Who was hung like an alpha baboon
And that is, perhaps
Why he lived with these chaps
In the jungles of east Cameroon

*

There was a young lady called Rene
Whose bosom just had to be seen
Her left boob was white
And so was the right
– but a blue one lay smack in between!

*

There was a young girl from Kildare
Who hadn't a great deal of hair
In fact, it was said
There was less on her head
Than there was on the old you know where

*

There was a young girl called Agrippa
Who took up a job as a stripper
To spice up her show
She'd reveal a tame crow
– and then a new use for a kipper

Oh, the curse of that gross masturbation!
The evil that stalks the whole nation
Coz let's not be fools…
In homes and in schools
It outstrips the use of PlayStation

*

There was a young chappie from Harridge
Who was not well prepared for his marriage
In fact, I've heard said
It was only when wed
That he learnt of his wife's undercarriage

*

The manhood of randy Dave Harris
(when rock-hard like plaster of Paris)
Could stay smooth and sleek
Though 'submerged' for a week
So he called it his 'pink-hued Polaris'

*

There was a young fellow from Kent
Whose penis was horribly bent
He could not easily bonk
But when climbing Mont Blanc
It did actually help his descent

There was a young chappie called Ollie
Who some said was right off his trolley
And my God they were right
When one dark stormy night
He eloped with his pet border collie

*

There was a young man from Berlin
Who thought bonking was just a great sin
And for crying out loud!
He was so well endowed
He could easily have topped Errol Flynn

*

There was a rich woman from Fleet
Who was not what you'd call just petite
Both her home there in Hants
And what lived in her pants
Were described as her large country seat

*

Young Tommy spoke fluent Punjabi
And ate only rice and kohlrabi
But his love of young boys
And his use of sex toys
Required him to leave Abu Dhabi

There was a young fellow called Tony
Who was known as the ultimate phoney
He acted the stud
But his acting was dud
Coz this 'stallion' was more like a pony

*

There was a young lady called Nancy
Who tickled young Geraldine's fancy
Yes, the two were a pair
And a tickle down there
Would see them both getting romancy

*

There was this young woman, Miss Worth
Who loved *saucisson, veau* and rare *boeuf*
In fact, one could say
She loved all things *Francais*
And that didn't exclude *soixante-neuf*

*

There was a young fellow called Vittof
Who once watched a girl get her kit off
When down to her skin
He then hurried straight in
And attempted to chew what he'd bit off

There was a young man from Bordeaux
Who paraded in just a *chapeau*
But not any more
Since he stepped out the door
And his penis got pecked by a crow

*

There was a young man from the Tyne
Who worshipped the god, Calvin Klein
In his pants he believed
And that's why he thieved
The four pairs that were hung on my line

*

There was a young man called Isaiah
Who once set a convent on fire
It's said it was done
With the help of a nun
As a way to ignite her desire

*

There was a young woman named Laura
Whose 'best friend' was called Isadora
And I'm certain of that
Coz I once heard them chat
About something that ends in 'majora'

There was a young chappie called Ben
Who bonked girls again and again
He wore women out
Coz without any doubt
The cock craved it more than the hen

*

Young Pretty Boy Joe's first arraignment
Was followed by years of containment
As soon as in clink
He did more than just think
That he might be the new entertainment!

*

There was a young woman called Frea
Who liked to make love in a Kia
Her partners were free
To explore A to Zee
– but were not ever let in the rear

*

The ears of a guy called Nathaniel
Were like those that you'd find on a spaniel
His todger was more
Like you'd find on a boar
(and not in a standard sex manual)

There was a young student from Herm
Who had only twenty-three sperm
He'd had a lot more
But that was before
The start of the Michaelmas term

*

There was a young man from Berlin
Whose tool was improbably thin
In fact, I've heard said
That his partners in bed
Couldn't tell when the damn thing was in

*

There was a young man from Port Said
Whose libido was famous worldwide
It was only a shame
That despite his great fame
He was grossly obese and one-eyed

*

There was a young woman called Nina
Who fell for a beauty called Tina
This 'Tine' had it all
Including one ball
And a full-sized arousable wiener

There was a young lady from Pinner
Whose sex life was like a large dinner
And that is to say
That once every day
She'd quite like to get a lot in 'er

*

There was a young girl from Capri
Who went for a buck-naked ski
It didn't quite last
As she slipped going fast
But she did get a thrill from a tree

*

There was a young creep named Delors
Who spied through the keyholes of doors
And that's how he found
That all housewives were bound
To keep certain stuff in their drawers

*

There was a young woman called Foley
Whose parents were pious and holy
And that's probably why
She was painfully shy
And in bed it all happened so slowly

There was a young girl from Verdun
Who went off to be trained as a nun
The first things she learnt
Was a bra could be burnt
And that candles were not made for fun

*

So cold is a woman called Lisa
That she can't even melt a Malteser
In fact, I admit
That (without any kit)
Even Clooney has failed to unfreeze her

*

There was a young fellow called Jake
Who once made an awful mistake
When in bed did he find
That the date whom he'd dined
Was in no way a duck but a drake

*

There was a young lady called Doris
Whose passion lay with her clit-oris
She caressed it most days
– and in all sorts of ways –
And she gave it a name – which was 'Boris'

There is this young girl called Priscilla
Who's as cute as a new-born chinchilla
But when taken to bed
She behaves, it's been said
Like one's neighbourhood nympho Godzilla

*

There was a young lady called Laura
Who wanted all men to adore her
Which is probably why
On a bed she would lie
And invite them to come and explore her

*

There once was a fellow called Rocky
Who started off life as a jockey
But with too many spills
He turned for his thrills
To professional naked mixed hockey

*

Our old Toby had sired seven daughters
And they later became news reporters
But the news of the day
I am delighted to say
Is they all have fantastic hind-quarters

There was a young lady called Mya
With a libido that couldn't be higher
There were so many men
Who had 'entered her den'
But alas they could not satisfy her

*

There was a young escort called Rita
Who did *not* want her clients to cheat her
So, with the help of a mate
She first set up a rate
Then fixed herself up with a meter

*

Young Jack, with the help of a friend
Would a brick from his penis suspend
His ambition, you see
Was not one brick but three
– and he did pull it off in the end

*

There was a young woman from Derry
Who once met this fellow called Gerry
Her feelings for fruit
Were extremely acute
But she did let him soon pop her cherry

There was a young girl from Angola
Who quite often used Coca Cola
It gave boys consent
– if used as a scent
And painted on each areola

*

There was a young woman called Brenda
Who was not very sure of her gender
Then a man came her way
And the doubt went away
Just as soon as he'd twanged that suspender…

*

There was a young hunter who came
To believe he could take this young dame
With her legs-apart stance
And her absence of pants
He formed the strong view she was game

*

There is a young girl who adores
Getting down on the floor on all fours
Before adopting this pose
She takes off all her clothes
Or sometimes no more than her drawers

There was a young woman called Lena
Who got screwed in a purple Cortina
She'd not known the big brute
But his bolas were cute
So she'd guessed he was from Argentina

*

There was a young man from Moncrief
Whose todger was armed with sharp teeth
Well, strangely enough
It put women off
But it did help him once catch a thief…

*

Young Jim was a gangster and rotten
All the gains that he'd got were ill-gotten
And the only one thing
That would tame this crime king
Was a girl in white pants made of cotton

*

There was a young woman who said
That she didn't much want to get wed
Coz marriage, she'd heard
Was like getting interred
(and one stopped having fun in a bed)

Kim's entrance on court won applause
Then her playing earned waves of loud roars
But this noisy acclaim
Was not for her game
But because she was not wearing drawers

*

There once was a lady called Poll
Who found a new use for her broll
To her husband's chagrin
She stabbed it right in
His brand-new inflatable doll

*

There was a young man who became
A girl with a quite different name
There were changes as well
To the way her clothes fell
– and her pants drawer was never the same

*

There was a young girl from Qatar
Who was quite often out of her bra
Her pants came off too
Coz between me and you
Her libido was well over par

There was a young gymnast called Dot
Who could do things that others could not
She could even do flips
With her hands on her hips
While a man put his coin in her slot

*

There was a young woman from Greece
Who went for a walk in a fleece
That is all that she wore
Not a single stitch more
And she thus caused a breach of the peace

*

There was a young woman called Kay
Who quite liked to have it away
In fact, so much so
That as far as I know
She did it six times every day

*

There was a young farmer from Stroud
Who was basically far too endowed
If he walked in a field
Then its fortune was sealed
Coz the whole thing would end up deep-ploughed

There was a young girl from Hong Kong
Whose legs put the ding into dong
Their shape was sublime
Their skin simply fine
And they ended right next to a thong

*

There once was a randy old goat
Who'd seduced this young girl on his boat
But when down on the deck
He got just a stiff neck
Coz his Viagra got stuck in his throat

*

Young Fanny was not very pleased
With a name that just meant she was teased
So a pussy was bought (!)
Coz with this she just thought
That her hurt might be finally eased…

*

There was a young chappie called Keith
Who'd attack bras and pants with his teeth
And this, he would say
Was much the best way
To find out what lay underneath

The woman who won Miss Australia
Had been garbed in elaborate regalia
– with a small design flaw
Which is why we all saw
Almost all of Miss A's genitalia

*

There was a young girl from Montrose
Who kept fit by touching her toes
But I have to confide
That she did this outside
And without wearing any damn clothes…

*

Young Jenny had not learnt to squat
It was something she'd failed at a lot
So relief would entail
A loo, pot or pail
On which she could rest her small bot

*

There was a young lady from Skye
Whose interest in sex toys was high
Whether hinged, ridged or plain
Or glass, steel or cane
She'd give every one a good try

There was a young laddie from Crewe
Whose 'transactions' with ladies were few
In fact, they were none
And all he had done
Was once get a full-frontal view

*

Young Tim was a tense lonely elf
When he pulled down a book from a shelf
This 'Book of Sex Acts'
Taught him how to relax
And he's so much now feeling himself

*

There was this young guy called Obama
Whose penis was shaped like a hammer
It scared girls away
From the thought of a lay
But it did cure one girl of her stammer

*

There is a young girl from Devizes
Who loves to wear different disguises
And especially one
Loosely based on a nun
– that first shocks one and then traumatizes

There was a young girl from Detroit
With some failings that men would exploit
Coz when doing such chores
As securing her drawers
She was simply not very adroit

*

There was a young girl called Maxine
Whose aim was to be quite obscene
To achieve such an end
Her whole self she would lend
And she'd even do stuff with her spleen!

*

There was a young girl from Romania
Who for ten quid would dress up and 'train' yer
In her tight leather shorts
She would teach you all sorts
And, if you did well, she would cane yer

*

There was a young man from Manila
Whose wife – well, he could not fulfil her
But what could he do?
He was four foot and two
– and she was the size called 'gorilla'

An Aussie young lady would wonder
Why it was that her suitors all shunned her
Til a friend pointed out
That without any doubt
They'd all hoped that they'd see her down under

*

There was a young witch called Yvonne
Whose usual response was a 'non'
But come a full moon
And you'd find very soon
That her pants and resolve had both gone

*

There was a young man from Carlisle
Who hadn't had sex for a while
So he had to make do
With an open-toed shoe
And a remodelled lever-arch file

*

There was a young girl from Sao Tome
Who thought of herself as Salome
She would slowly dispose
Of her layers of clothes
And what lay underneath she'd then show me

There was a young woman called Emma
Who was faced with a special dilemma
Should she try to seduce
Gemma's boyfriend called Bruce
– or propose a quick threesome with Gemma?

*

There was a young girl who was stout
And who suffered from spells of self-doubt
But although a plump wimp
When her boyfriend went limp
She knew how to straighten him out

*

There was a young girl called Simone
Who quite liked to be on her own
What then she would do
Nobody quite knew
But she did often let out a groan

*

There was a young man from Stranraer
Who with girls would drive off in his car
And then he would say
'Shall we go all the way?'
– but rarely they'd go very far

There was a young girl who was found
At the top of a hill on the ground
It seems that a youth
(who was very uncouth)
Had intended to get on her mound

*

There was a young lady from Rouen
Who rather liked food she could chew on
She also liked men
And again and again
She'd retire to the bed that she'd screw on

*

There was a young lady called Sally
Who with wrinklies would get very pally
Despite being old
With Viagra, I'm told
Their stiffness was right up her alley

*

There was a young chappie from Tonga
Who was known for the length of his donger
At rest it was more
Than two foot and four
'*En garde*' it was half a yard longer

Young Titania was dined at the Ritz
And loved both the food and the glitz
Her host loved them too
But between me and you
He more loved the thought of Tit's bits

*

There was a young man from Helsinki
Whose sex life was all sorts of kinky
It had to be so
Coz as far as I know
His winkler was not even dinky

*

There was an old man who was irked
At the poor way his manhood now worked
But a pill did he find
– of a marvellous kind –
And up now his manhood has perked

*

There was a young woman called Gert
Whose boyfriend designed her best skirt
And I have heard it said
That before they got wed
He did have a hand in her shirt

Young Tim was a wil-o'-the-wisp
And a nephew of old Quentin Crisp
So he soon learnt to say
'I'm really not gay
It's just that I've got this queer lisp'

*

There was a young girl from Penzance
Who her sex life she sought to enhance
She did this with flirts
And with very short skirts
And by giving up wearing her pants

*

King Midas, for years, it's been told
Turned all that he touched into gold
And it follows from this
When he went for a piss
Someone else had to be there to hold

*

There was a young girl with big eyes
But with boobs of a similar size
Like eggs cut in half
They made people laugh
So she christened them Morecombe and Wise

There was a young girl called Matilda
Who married a well-endowed builder
He first won her heart
(with his oversized part)
When he took her and more than just filled her

*

There was a gay lady called Jenny
Whose girlfriends were almost too many
Then her tryst with those ewes
Hit the Nine O'clock News
And she soon found she didn't have any

*

There was a Newcastle supporter
Who did what he shouldn't have oughta
Between you and me
It involved some ripe Brie
And the 'help' of the chairman's fit daughter

*

There was a young woman called Hunt
Who tried this impossible stunt
She broke her left thumb
Put a dent in her bum
And her nipples are now back to front

There is a young fellow called Trevor
Who's not what you'd call very clever
But he's nobody's fool
When it comes to his tool
Which is huge and can stay up forever

*

There was a young whore from Honshu
Who had this extensive tattoo
I have heard reports
T'was a menu of sorts
And it showed all the things she would do

*

Young Bessy was such a damn diva
That her boyfriend was planning to leave her
But this Canada guy
He just couldn't say 'bye
To young Bessy's incredible beaver

*

There once was a girl who believed
That by kissing a boy she'd conceived
So with nothing to lose
She indulged in three screws
And she's now feeling rather aggrieved

There was a young nun so devout
In her faith there was no room for doubt
But there was room for sin
Like a nightcap of gin
And some playtime before 'candles out'

*

There was a young thicko called Scotty
Who was not having luck getting totty
Then he thought he'd be saved
With what many girls craved
And had implants installed in his botty!

*

There was a young girl from Hong Kong
Who once wore a very thin thong
It was so very thin
It soon forced its way in
– to a place where it didn't belong

*

There once was a girl called Lolita
Whose boyfriend knew well how to treat her
I won't tell you how
At least not for now
But he did use a cane carpet beater

There is this old geezer called Ben
Who gets to have girls now and then
He'd like to have more
But it's quite hard to score
When they learn he's one hundred and ten

*

There was a young girl called Camilla
Whose boyfriend had promised to thrill her
But it was not to be
As between you and me
The poor chap could not even fill her

*

There was a young woman called Clare
Who had only one pubic hair
Of course this did mean
That her charms could be seen
When she chose to parade wholly bare

*

There was a young chap from Al-Qaeda
Whose wife just got wider and wider
So fat did she grow
(both up top and below)
That the poor chap could not get inside her

There was a young Rambo called Treasure
Whose job was to give women pleasure
With a mouth made to kiss
He was perfect for this
(and his todger was just beyond measure)

*

I have quite often heard it opined
When a man on his own is confined
That the way he'll react
Is to seek out an act
That in due course will make him go blind

*

There is this young girl called Teresa
Who'll do just what you want so to please yer
But mind how you go
Coz I happen to know
That the last guy she pleased had a seizure

*

There was a young man who just knew
That not everything girls say is true
And as for those groans
(as in orgasmic moans)
Well, they're just what they think they should do…

There was a young guy from Dunblane
Who was not what you'd call very sane
In fact, I have heard
That to pick up a bird
He'd first go and hire a damn crane

*

There was a young lady called Jade
Who took up a time-honoured trade
It called for blonde hair
And some cheap underwear
And long hours with her legs widely splayed

*

A musician who lived in Caracas
One day found himself in a fracas
The fighting was tough
And quite tough enough
To cause him to lose his maracas

*

There was a young fellow called Sam
Who styled himself 'Ramrod the Ram'
But those girls who all knew
What it was he could do
Rechristened him 'Limp-rod the Lamb'

There was a young chappie called Ken
Whose penis was two foot and ten
For most of the time
He controlled it just fine
But it did trip him up now and then

*

There was a young lady from Bute
Whose interest in balls was acute
When meeting a stud
Just as soon as she could
She'd go for his low-hanging fruit

*

There was a young fellow called Sid
Who'd done what he shouldn't have did
– with a girl and an owl
And a soaking-wet towel
And the payment – in change – of a quid

*

There was a young girl in a dorm
Who was woken one night by a storm
What she went and did then
With a candle and pen
Was not what you'd say was the norm

There was a young man from Vancouver
Who found a new use for a hoover
Just think of a suck
The back end of a duck
Then add in a Heimlich Manoeuver…

*

When Annie's libido was started
It was not for the weak or fainthearted
It would lovers so strain
That they'd end up in pain
– or as one of the dearly departed

*

There was a hot girl called Lorraine
Who liked to eat pies with champagne
The pies she would scoff
The champers she'd quaff
– and then she'd have sex (with a cane)

*

There was a young woman called Winnie
Who had this phenomenal innie
It looked like a purse
With its opening transverse
– like the engine they put in a Mini

There was a young man from Burundi
Who liked to have sex on a Sunday
– with a manhood so strong
And inclined to stay long
It quite often stretched into Monday

*

It was bad for a lady called Gunnel
When a flashlight slipped into her 'funnel'
But of hell she was spared
When a doctor declared
There was light at the end of the tunnel…

*

There was a 'young girl' made of plastic
With inserts of well-oiled elastic
Her purpose was clear
But I tell you, my dear
Her offerings were less than fantastic

*

There was a young girl who confessed
To having a much enhanced chest
In fact, I recall
They had had to install
Thirteen kilos in each single breast

There was a young girl from Renfrew
Whose lovers all said 'canna do'
(There were so many hairs
On the poor girl's downstairs
That they just couldn't find their way through)

*

There was a young man called Legrande
Who could pleasure himself on demand
But the pleasure, it ceased
When his member, he greased
And the whole thing got well out of hand

*

There was this young girl who was Greek
Who made sounds that were really unique
For who else could evoke
While receiving a poke
The enjoyment of bubble and squeak?

*

There was a cute slave girl in Rome
Who worked in a rich Roman's home
His name was Tiberius
She sent him delirious
And sometimes she made 'Tiber' foam…

There was a young girl quite unsure
Of the strength of her young pelvic floor
But when pounded real hard
By a big Irish Guard
She just knew it could take a lot more

*

There was a young chappie called Ben
Who was different from most other men
When it came to the game
That has 'sex' for its name
He would not play the cock *or* the hen

*

Young Simon was seen as quite crackers
For sharing his flat with alpacas
He'd be knocked to the floor
Head-butted galore
And quite often kicked in the knackers

*

There was a young girl from Madrid
Who employed a device that she hid
No one was quite sure
What she used the thing for
But I did hear it most easily slid

There was a young woman from Keele
Whose fine sense of touch was surreal
After only a week
At a men's club in Speke
She could tell all the members by feel

*

There was a young girl who was dowdy
And who married a middle-aged Saudi
In some ways she won
But for sex and for fun
– the outlook was more than just cloudy

*

There was a young Tesco shelf-packer
Whose Christmas could not have been blacker
His girlfriend, my dear,
Threw him out on his ear
And he then had to pull his own cracker

*

There was a young lady called Charlotte
Who worked all her life as a harlot
But with crowds on the streets
And a love of back seats
She would ply all her trade in a car lot

Young Jenny's bikini was white
And made very thin to be light
Which is why (happily)
When she rose from the sea
She provided a see-through delight

*

There was a young fellow called Neil
Whose penis was fashioned from steel
As one would expect
It was always erect
But that still left it far from ideal

*

There was an old man who would drool
At the girls as they swam in a pool
But before they were through
– and with teaching to do –
He had to get back to his school

*

There was this Greek god guy called Zeus
Whose actions were often abstruse
Having once played a swan
(for Queen Leda to con)
He then went and gave her a goose

There was a young lady called Pippa
Who took up a job as a stripper
I know for a fact
She had fish in her act
– and one tiny but carefully placed kipper

*

There was a young girl who liked trees
But more so her partners to please
In pursuit of this cause
When buying new drawers
She would check how they looked round her knees

*

There was a young lady from Cowes
Who all menfolk she sought to arouse
She did this with smiles
And with all sorts of wiles
And by wearing a tight-fitting blouse

*

There was a young man from Nepal
Who sadly had no balls at all
He'd started with two
But he'd worn them both through
With the help of a girl from Porthcawl

There was a young priest who would say
That the limerick had now had its day
So who'd have foreseen
That by humping the dean
He would help it to not go away

*

There was a nude man called Al Core
Who plugged in a circular saw
He put it to use
With his manhood still loose
And now Al's not a man anymore

*

Young Mary had pants that were sheer
(so sheer they were almost not here)
And of course what that meant
Is when over she bent
You could get a clear view of her rear

*

There was a small woman from Britain
Who with felines was seriously smitten
She loved her own cat
But I have to say that…
Her pussy was more like a kitten

On holidays Jim wore his shorts
When he swam or he played different sports
But their failure to hide
What was lurking inside
Got him banned from at least five resorts

*

There was a young girl from Bermuda
Who once met a huge barracuda
What she then let it do
I will not tell to you
But it could not have been any cruder

*

There was a young man from the East
Who went to a big wedding feast
One bridesmaid addressed him
And when she caressed him
The room in his Y-fronts decreased

*

With grass skirts the girls would entrance
All the sailors from England and France
Then the lawnmower came
And it wasn't the same
Coz they all had to start wearing pants

There was a young chappie called Pete
Who preferred to make love on his feet
On his front he was poor
On his back even more
And with upright they couldn't compete

*

Young Karen's degree was first class
And so too, I am told, was her arse
But her arse was of use
(to her boyfriend, Big Bruce)
While her so-called degree was a farce

*

There was a young chappie called Gerry
Who attractive to girls wasn't very
But then he'd reveal
His awesome real deal
Which would earn him a bite of their cherry

*

There was a young woman from Norway
Who didn't think much about foreplay
Then Ken came around
And that's when she found
How much it could open her doorway

There was a young man from Seville
Who 'went' with a girl up a hill
Jack was his name
Lust was his game
And the girl he went up was named Jill

*

There was a young man who loved Blur
– and a 'jewel' that is covered in fur
(It's not often on show
But what you should know
Is its namesake will quite often purr)

*

There was a young dancer whose goal
Was to find for herself a good role
But she had to say no
To a place in a show
When she found that they'd not cleaned the pole

*

There was a young girl named Celeste
Who had this odd thing on one breast
Shaped like a ripple
Above her left nipple
It played Auld Lang Syne when depressed

There was a young woman from Kew
Whose boyfriends were far less than few
The reason, it's said
Is when taken to bed
She had rather much less than a clue

*

There was a young man from Turin
Who was once halfway out and half in
At which point he said
'Do you think we should wed
Coz this might constitute a real sin?'

*

There was a young man from Dunkirk
Who was shocked when his thing wouldn't work
But then he recalled
That if ever it stalled
He just needed to give it a jerk

*

There was a young lady from Harrow
Whose inter-thigh gap was too narrow
So her maidenhood stayed
Until she was laid
By a guy with a tool like an arrow

There was a young girl who it's said
Wore drawers that were grey or dull red
But I know I am right
If her drawers were plain white
She expected to end up in bed

*

Nick's manhood would normally harden
When it got near a trimmed lady's garden
But I have to declare
If the garden was bare
It would quite often put a whole yard on

*

There was a young man with a tractor
Who used it to kidnap an actor
In no way, my dear
Was his motive that clear
But his gayness was probably a factor

*

A long-serving whore from Shanghai
Just knew that her end was quite nigh
So she set out to find
A coffin designed
In the shape of a capital Y

There was a young girl from Seattle
Who developed a serious rattle
Some said it would halt
With a man in her vault
But I think that was just tittle-tattle

*

There once was a lady called Phipps
Who had the most flexible hips
She could 'bend them in two'
Then poke her head through
And in that way then kiss her own lips

*

There was a horse rider called Pippa
Who was prone to an urge that would grip her
When out for a ride
She'd expose her backside
And then ask a companion to whip her

*

There was a girl motorbike rider
Who learnt to take bends ever wider
The reason, you see
Was the men principally
Coz she quite liked to have them inside her

Fair Cheryl, when young, she was told
'Orgasms are better than gold
They cost not a dime
They are 'there' any time
And they're quite often fine to behold'

*

There was a young fellow called Haggard
Who was known as a bit of a blaggard
But the girls didn't care
Coz they were all well aware
That in bed he could bloody well sh… shine like a star

*

There was a French man from Verdun
Who didn't think sex was much fun
Then one steamy night
It all came just right
When he switched from an *une* to an *un*

*

There was this young man from Kuwait
Who of wives wanted no less than eight
But he stopped at just two
Coz between me and you
His performance in bed was third-rate

There was a young fellow called Yuri
Who recounted this breath-taking story
It revolved round the fact
That an oral sex act
Can be heard on the last Jackanory

*

There was a young woman from Devon
Whose 'men in a day' count was seven
But that was before
On one cricket-team tour
When her record shot up to eleven

*

Young Ingrid who'd once lived in Stoke
Kept herself well away from most folk
But then Ken 'breached her walls'
– and found she had balls
Yes, our Ingrid was really a bloke…

*

There was this big hunk of a Dane
Who made love to a girl from Bahrain
And without telling tales
He soon bought her some rails
– coz when started she went like a train

There was a young woman from Bonn
Whose 'sex switch' was always switched on
Like a powered device
She would always entice
And would hump 'til her juice had all gone

*

There was a young girl called Loretta
Who was known as a bit of a fretter
She fretted so much
She'd not even touch
A man's pride and joy if he let her

*

There was a young man called Pierre
Whose wife made the poor sod despair
When offered romance
She would keep on her pants
And instead eat a chocolate éclair

*

On the fruit farm of old farmer Vickers
Was a party he held for his pickers
This harvest event
Was held in a tent
And the dress code was 'come without knickers'

There was a young lady from Harborne
Who once snagged her blouse on a car horn
Well, that's what she said
To the guy whom she'd wed
To explain how she'd had her new bra torn

*

A young hussy was keen on those guys
Who had kit of an extra-large size
And just to be clear
What we're talkin' 'bout here
Is their kit that she'd cause to arise…

*

Young Steve who was born under Taurus
Once slept with a girl stegosaurus
When the steg then produced
Was when Steve then deduced
That the condom he'd worn had been porous

*

There was a small fellow called Kenneth
Whose libido was well past its zenith
So this will-o'-the-wisp
(with a terrible lisp)
Instead took to mixed table tennith

There was a young woman called Maude
Whose mind was improbably broad
She'd blow and she'd screw
She'd have me and have you
And she'd even have sex in a Ford

*

There was a young man called Marcel
Whose gender was quite hard to tell
He looked like a *beau*
But as far as I know
He more often seemed like a *belle*

*

There was an old warlock called Grumman
Who the forces of evil did summon
But not to get wealth
Or even good health
But instead just a nymph-like young woman

*

Young Mark the magician was fond
Of the use of *double entendre*
And what better way
To put this in play
Than to talk of the size of his wand

There was a young prince who liked beige
And encounters with boys underage
But his crimes came to light
On one dark moonless night
When his insert went in the wrong page

*

There was a young girl from Milan
Who wanted to change to a man
She wanted some balls
And to wear overalls
And to drive a white Ford Transit van

*

There was a young girl from Pamplona
Who was seen as a permanent loner
But then she met Nate
Whose male organ was great
(and Nate was a keen organ donor)

*

There was a young woman from Cowes
Who menfolk she sought to arouse
In pursuit of this cause
She more miniscule drawers
And always a transparent blouse

There was a young woman from Haiti
Who was more than decidedly matey
And that's why, they say
In the course of one day
The menfolk she bonked numbered eighty

*

There was a young batsman called Moore
Whose all-round performance was poor
In fact, I hear say
That if Moore didn't pay
The poor sod would just never score

*

There was a young chap called Carruthers
Whose tackle was not like his brother's
In fact, as I know
If observed from below
It looked rather more like his mother's

*

There was a young girl called Christine
Whose demeanour was soft and serene
But given the chance
(and an absence of pants)
She would soon act in ways quite obscene

There was a young girl called Rebecca
Who was known as a rare 'double-decker'
Coz as well as her 'it'
And above it a bit
Was a full-sized (and circumcised) pecker

*

There was a young man who could claim
That his manhood was just like his name
Coz his name, I can tell
Was Hugh Jandhungwell
– and his todger was truly the same

*

There once was a woman called Tessa
Who asked Father Joseph to bless her
But the padre misheard
Which is why, on his word
He proceeded to quickly undress her

*

There was a young girl called Svetlana
Who once took a trip to Guyana
Whilst there on her tour
She got nicked by the law
And charged with 'Abuse of banana'

There was a young fellow called Vaughn
Who'd spend hours every day watching porn
Not any old stuff
But just girls in the buff
Being rude with kohlrabi and Quorn

*

There was a young girl who'd rehearse
With a whip and with wants quite perverse
She loved in her act
Not her whip to be cracked
But instead what was quite the reverse

*

There was a young woman who knew
That of good men there were very few
And of those who were so
Even fewer would know
What it took for a memorable screw

*

There was a young woman who said
'I'd rather have sex than have bread
At the end of the day
A nice sarnie's OK
But it don't match a roll in a bed'

There once was a woman from Mali
Who was painted by Salvador Dali
He showed her as blue
And with two eyes askew
And a third one in place of her Charlie

*

There was a young bridegroom called Walter
Who'd picked up his bride in Gibraltar
As on their first date
He just couldn't wait
Which is why they had sex at the altar

*

There was a young lady from Hants
Who just yearned for a bit of romance
And if not true *amour*
Then at least rather more
Than 'Eh luv, what's this in yer pants?'

*

There was a young woman from Cowes
Who had a large hole in her blouse
And why it was there
(just between her large pair)
Was to let all the studs have a browse

There was a young lover called Billy
With a winner's rosette on his willy
The reason, you see
Just between you and me
Was he'd always come first with a filly

*

There once was a geezer called Noah
Whose wife was a bit of a goer
She loved to make love
With her husband above
But better when he was below her

*

There was a young woman from Dorking
Who adopted a posh way of talking
And so she would say
When she'd had it away
'One can't beat a jolly good forking'

*

There was a young man who designed
A free-standing woman's behind
Quite what it was for
He wasn't too sure
But he did keep it very well shined

There was a young servant who felt
That great was the hand he'd been dealt
With his master at war
With his wife he could score
(with the key to her chastity belt)

*

There was a young girl in some dread
Of where she might end up when dead
So she made up her mind
To be very kind
– and each night take someone to bed

*

There was a young man called Bob Hunt
Who planned to have sex in a punt
But he thought just in time
Of a terrible rhyme
– so he settled for just a long grunt

*

There was a young man on a ship
Whose girlfriend would willingly strip
But she'd soon then be gone
And, like a bet not put on
He'd have wasted a really hot tip

There was a young fellow from Brent
Whose manhood was horribly bent
It was all due, I learned
To a girl whom he'd spurned
And a bowl of quick-setting cement

*

There was a young fellow from Slough
Who once had this crush on a cow
It didn't last long
Coz the 'why' was all wrong
– though not quite as wrong as the 'how'

*

The girl of a paperback writer
Soon found that his work could delight her
He'd open real well
His action would gel
And his climax would always excite her

*

There was a poor girl who awoke
Lying next to an ugly nude bloke
She felt the same way
As she did on the day
That she heard her first Frankie Boyle joke

There is a young woman called Ginny
Who likes to have sex in a Mini
But this rather dictates
That she, like her mates
Is obliged to remain very skinny

*

There was a young climber called Dale
Who longed for his girlfriend to scale
She longed for it too
But I'm told that it's true
That his tackle would too often fail

*

There was a young fellow who spied
A girl coming in on the tide
When she got to the shore
He could see rather more
– and his decency curled up and died

*

There was a young girl who was faced
With the chance to remain truly chaste
But the chance it slipped by
With that hand on her thigh
And its owner so much to her taste

There was a young major called Bruce
Who once stuck his head in a noose
He wanted to die
And the true reason why
Was his privates were no bloody use

*

There was a young girl who had drawers
That she'd wear when performing her chores
But she also had pants
That were made for romance
(of the sort undertaken by whores)

*

There was a young lady called Hannah
Who was sweet and refined in her manner
But I happen to know
That a few years ago
She'd go all the way for a tanner

*

There was this young son of a farmer
Whose love life was full of real drama
– along with a goat
A rather nice stoat
And a short-sighted, warm-hearted llama

There were many fine girls at the dance
Whose 'skirt moves' could simply entrance
But without any doubt
The girl who stood out
Was the one who had come minus pants

*

There was a young man in Bangkok
Who suffered a rather big shock
Coz his date, Fifi Chen
Owned not just a hen
But a bloody great oversized cock

*

There once was a famous explorer
Who set off in search of new flora
But all that he found
Was a girl on the ground
And he named her 'Lobelia minora'

*

There was this old geezer who saw
That his prospects for sex were quite poor
But he put out a tweet
That his knob touched his feet
And these dumb birds turned up by the score

There was a young woman called Trump
Who boasted a well-rounded rump
But this rump, I declare
Was just down to some air
And the use of a pneumatic pump

*

There was a young woman from Frome
Who went for an intimate groom
The groomer was male
And the end of this tale
Is just what you'll no doubt assume

*

There was a young girl from Chicago
Whose boobs could be classed as bulk cargo
So huge were this pair
That when travelling by air
She'd have them sent on by Wells Fargo

*

There was a young woman called Brenda
Whose lover was thoughtful and tender
But every two days
He would 'take' her all ways
And he'd quite often even upend her

There was a young man from Nevada
Who was prone to a terrible ardour
When a girl said hello
His manhood would grow
– and soon things would get even harder

*

There was a young fellow called Tim
Who met this young girl at a gym
He found when in bed
(when her knickers were shed)
That she really did keep very trim

*

There was a young charmer called Neil
Whose member was just like an eel
It didn't have eyes
But it was a surprise
For all those who gave it a feel

*

There was a young lady called Sally
Who devoted her life to the ballet
She loved all the dance
And those men in tight pants
– and their clinches were right up her alley

Young Tilley could only despair
At the mass and the length of her hair
If only up top
There was such a fine mop
…instead of it all being down there

*

There was a young woman who pined
For a love who was rather refined
But when rough 'Stan the Stud'
Went and flashed his manhood
She thought she might just change her mind

*

There is this nice fellow called Piers
Who's been searching for over three years
What he's hoping to find
Are his 'two of a kind'
Which he lost when he sat on some shears

*

There was a young woman called Maisie
Whose knowledge of bonking was hazy
In fact, it was said
That her action in bed
Was as bad as a film by Scorsese

There was a young girl who liked grapes
And the fact that our cousins are apes
But what she liked best
Was to take off her vest
And mould her two boobs into shapes

*

There was a young girl from Australia
Who, with boys, was an absolute failure
Although she looked great
She could not get a date
Coz the poor girl was named Jenny Talia

*

There was a young fellow from Jeddah
Whose face would get redder and redder
This was due, I can state
To a girl from Kuwait
And would happen whenever he bed her

*

There were these young girl who had grounds
For declaring themselves out of bounds
The problem you see
Just between you and me
Was that men would stray on to their mounds

There was a young man from Torbay
Who liked having sex every day
With his wife not so keen
This would quite often mean
He'd be playing both home and away

*

There was a young man from Dumfries
Who with bras found them hard to release
So off they would come
O'er hips and o'er bum
– with the help of a handful of grease

*

There was a young man from Blantyre
Who once felt his balls were on fire
The reason for that
Was a load of hot fat
And the strength of a spurned woman's ire

*

The private was still dressed in serge
When consumed by a terrible urge
The court martial said
With the porn he'd been fed
He had always been just on the verge

There was a young whore called Brunhilda
Who'd do any damn sex for a guilder
If you'd only a sou
That would probably do
Just as long as the last time you'd thrilled her

*

There was a young woman from Hayes
Who performed the sex act several ways
But the one she like best
Was the one they called 'Test'
Coz this one could last for five days…

By the same author:

Brian's World Series

Brian on the Brahmaputra (with Sujan in the Sundarbans)
A Syria Situation
Sabah-taged
Cape Earth
Strip Pan Wrinkle (in Namibia and Botswana)
Crystal Balls and Moroccan Walls
Marmite, Bites and Noisy Nights (in Zambia)
The Country-cides of Namibia and Botswana
First Choose Your Congo
Absolutely Galápagos
Melanesia, Melancholia and Limericks
A Man A Plan A Canal Panama

The Renton Tenting Trilogy

Dumpiter
Ticklers
Lollipop

Light-bites

Eggshell in Scrambled Eggs
Crats
The A-Z of Stuff

www.davidfletcherbooks.co.uk

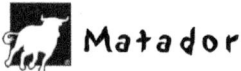

For exclusive discounts on Matador titles,
sign up to our occasional newsletter at
troubador.co.uk/bookshop